D1713025

TABLE OF CONTENTS

CARDBOARD
CARPENTRY

by *Janet & Alex D'Amato*
Foreword by *Morton Thompson, Ed.D.*

THE
LION
PRESS

FOREWORD

This is a book to help children make interesting and simple creations from materials which can be found in the home. Most of the projects need only scissors, paste, crayons, poster or finger paints, pipe cleaners, soda straws, clips, staples etc., plus cardboard cartons and boxes. The many colorful toys and other items shown will challenge the imagination of the young and will provide them with a medium of creating attractive objects for themselves, their family and their friends.

This is also a work book on cardboard art and cut-outs, developed as a resource guide for elementary school teachers, camping and youth group leaders, parents and volunteers in educational and recreation programs who need indoor or "rainy-day" activities as part of their programs. The projects in this book are excellent for those times when children may be bed-patients recovering from an illness. Even then they can profit by the interest created and the skills learned.

The projects featured are not passive "punch-out" die-cut assemblies but require a simple and active participation. The child can learn and exercise basic skills and procedures useful in later forms of handicraft; tracing patterns, cutting on lines, etc., and can develop an imagination for color and design. Children also need the opportunity to use scissors and the other "adult" tools involved and to develop a sense of carefulness and responsibility. However, the leader should always stress safety and respect for the effectiveness of good equipment.

"Learning can be fun" is no platitude when handicraft is involved and the primary purpose of this book is to provide a guide to and suggestions for entertaining and creative projects that have special values for children.

Morton Thompson, Ed.D.
Recreation Consultant
National Recreation and Park Association

INTRODUCTION

You may not realize how much good cardboard is thrown away at your house. Once a box or container is empty, shake out any crumbs or remaining food. Boxes that contained cookies, cereal, crackers, or facial tissue are made of lightweight cardboard that is easy to cut and handle. The cardboard that comes in shirts from the laundry often is of similiar weight. When instructions simply say use "cardboard" we mean this type, unless stated otherwise.

You can make all these projects using simple materials that are usually found in any average home. Most items need scissors, paste, poster paints, and perhaps pipe cleaners, soda straws or staples.

If paint or paste will not hold on the surface you are working with, rub the surface with liquid detergent and then paint. Otherwise use crayons or felt-tipped markers for color. Often household cement will hold on difficult surfaces better than paste. Many joinings can be held with transparent sticky tape.

Many pages in this book have designs or plans that are to be transferred to the material you are going to use. You can do this easily by placing a piece of carbon paper under the drawing and on top of the cardboard. Then, pressing firmly, trace the outline, with an old ball-point pen that has run dry. Since the pen has no ink in it, it will not mark the book as would a pencil and it will make a good impression through the carbon paper. Another method is to place a thin sheet of paper over the drawing. Use a paper thin enough to see the lines underneath and trace the outline directly on the paper. When you have finished either paste the paper directly on the cardboard or use carbon paper as above.

Now that you've read the general instructions, look around you and collect as many different kinds of boxes as possible — little ones, big ones, all shapes. Beginning with these drab little boxes and by using patience and a lot of imagination, you will be able to create lovely objects that your family and friends will admire and you will have a lot of fun making.

Come and join us on a short trip into the wonderful world of cardboard boxes and cartons.

How To Make
Cardboard Toys and Games

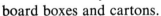

There are a great variety of things to do and make using the cardboard cut from lightweight boxes or shirt boards.

Here is a way to make a simple and attractive mobile. Cut out several pictures of the lively animals and characters on your cereal boxes. Tie threads through the tops of each. Tie to bottom of hanger at different lengths. Hang in your room. Presto — you have a mobile.

Girls can make their own paper dolls. Cut pictures from old magazines or newspapers. Drawings advertising bathing suits or petticoats are best. Mount the picture of the girl on cardboard, and cut out. To make clothes for her, make a pattern by using lightweight paper you can see through. Lay over doll and trace around waist and shoulders and skirt line. Draw on tabs to hold dress in place. Use this pattern to cut dresses out of different colored papers. Decorate.

Miniature Menagerie

Trace the animal heads and backs at the bottom of this page onto cardboard. When dry, cut out. Paste onto empty thread spools. Using these as patterns you can make as many animals as you like for your menagerie.

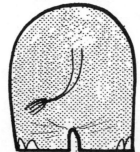

Make Your Own Mosaics—Cardboard Tessera

Tessera is an old Latin word that means a square piece of stone, ivory or wood. Since you are using cardboard you can call it cardboard tessera. Boxes are printed in many bright and colorful designs, sometimes even gold. To make tiles, cut ¼″ strips and then snip into squares. Pictures of products such as cookies or spaghetti make interesting textured tiles.

Draw a rough design on a plain piece of cardboard. Here are two picture suggestions. Coloring books are good places to look for ideas too. Spread paste on a small area at a time. Set tiles in place. Cut and trim your "tiles" when needed to fit design.

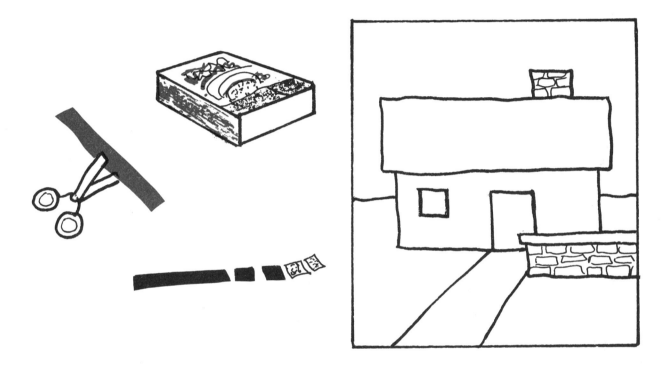

Make a Kicking Monster Monkle

Trace these two pages and paste on cardboard. When dry, color as outlandishly as you please. Cut out and punch holes where shown. Attach legs and wings to body with four paper fasteners. Cut a piece of string 20″ long. Overlap tops of legs and tie string through at x point, leaving 10″ hanging below. Tie the other end of the string through wings at x as shown. Continue up through hole in top of head. Hold Monkle at his side; pull either top or bottom string and watch him move.

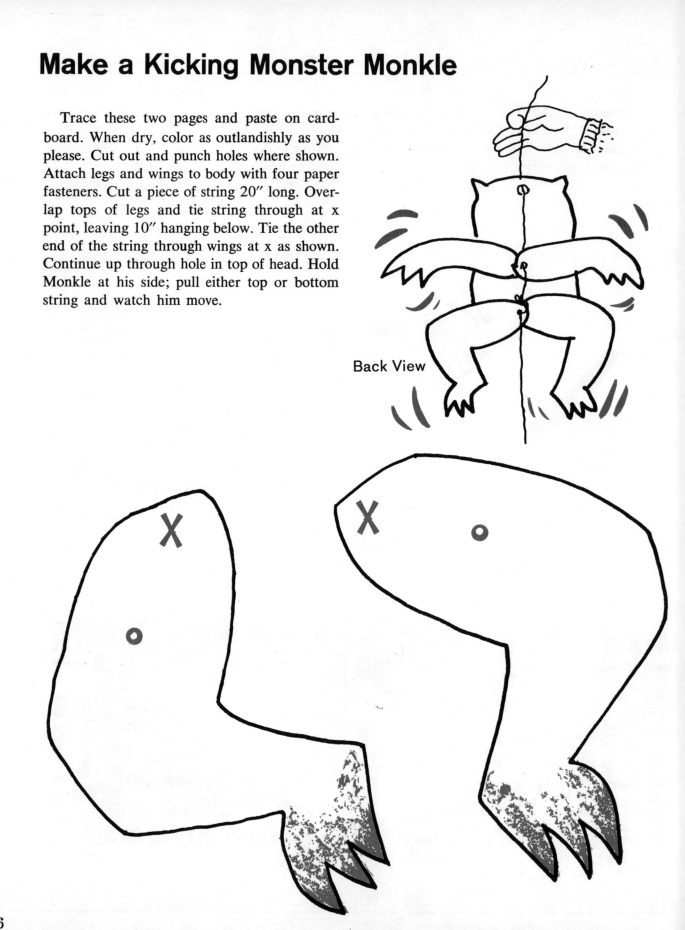

Back View

X

X

7

Make a Bang! Bang!

Use a panel of a cereal box. Cut apart from box and fold in half horizontally.

Trace gun shape from this page and transfer it to your folded piece, making sure fold is in the right place. Cut both sides of cardboard together. Trace pattern of "Bang" on a folded sheet of lightweight writing paper. Cut out. Open up and paste one side of tab to one side of gun on shaded area as shown. Let dry thoroughly. Then fold "Bang" into gun and paste other tab in place. Let dry.

To make a loud "Bang," raise your gun in the air and bring it down sharply. For best results, hold gun handle slightly open to allow paper to flip out noisily.

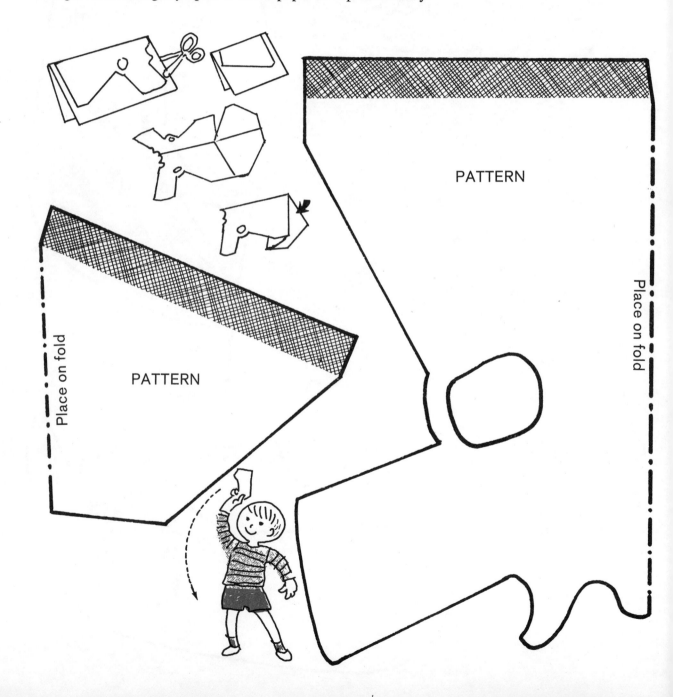

PATTERN

PATTERN

Place on fold

Place on fold

Clothespins Farm

Trace off the patterns on this and the following pages for additional animals. Now pull out this page. Paste one side of sheep on a piece of cardboard. Fold around bottom of sheep and paste other side. When dry, cut out carefully. Clip on two clothespins as shown for legs (colored area). See how well he stands up.

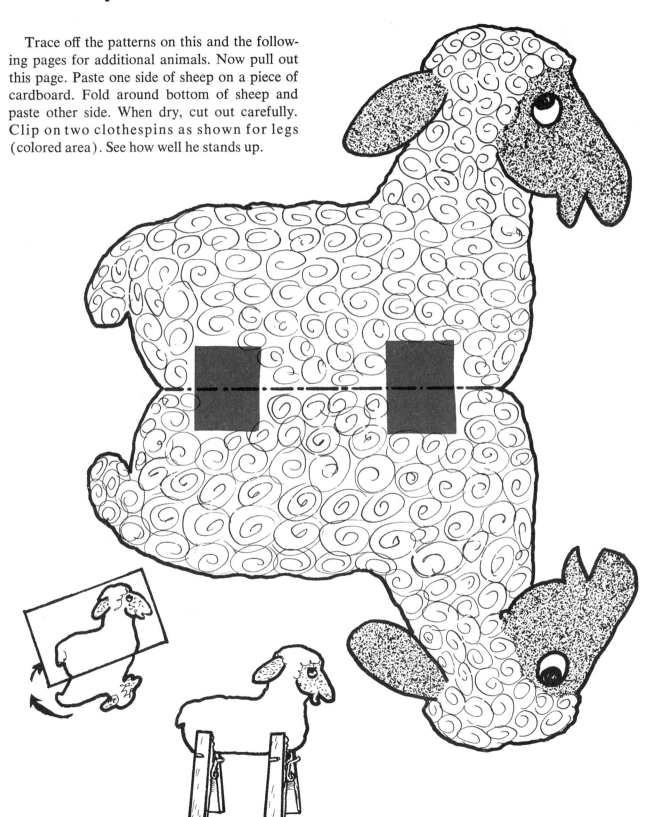

Trace the patterns of the animals on these two pages onto different colored cardboards. Draw eyes and mouths with felt pens. Cut out and attach clothespins for legs. By using these animals for size you can make a complete farmyard.

A Dragon For Dragging

Trace the head and tail on cardboard. Cut out. Fold head piece where shown, making bottom jaw underneath. Use body pattern to cut out body shapes. Cut as many as you like, from different colored boxes. Cut small snips of soda straws about ¼″ long, or use macaroni of the same shape.

Cut a piece of string or yarn about a yard long. Thread on a heavy needle. Tie end to tail piece. Now start stringing, alternating each body piece with a piece of straw. When you have a nice long dragon, thread string through back of head and up his nose. Tie at his nose leaving a long piece so you can drag him around.

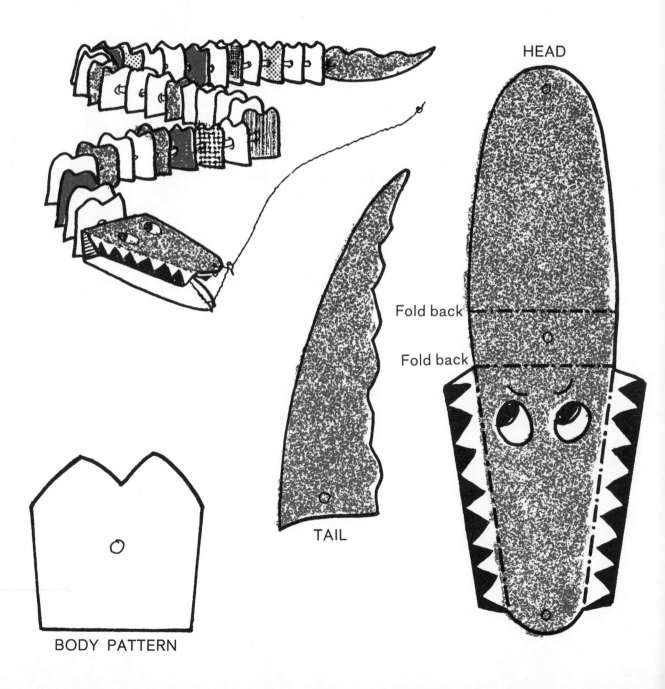

HEAD

Fold back

Fold back

TAIL

BODY PATTERN

"Beaky" The Balancing Bird

Here is a bird that loves to perch on your finger. Trace shape below onto cardboard. Color and draw beak, eyes, and feathers on both sides. Cut him out carefully.

Tape a penny to the end of each wing. Place "Beaky" carefully on the end of your finger; balance him, and he will sit there. He'll even perch on the top of your pencil. Try balancing "Beaky" in other places around the house.

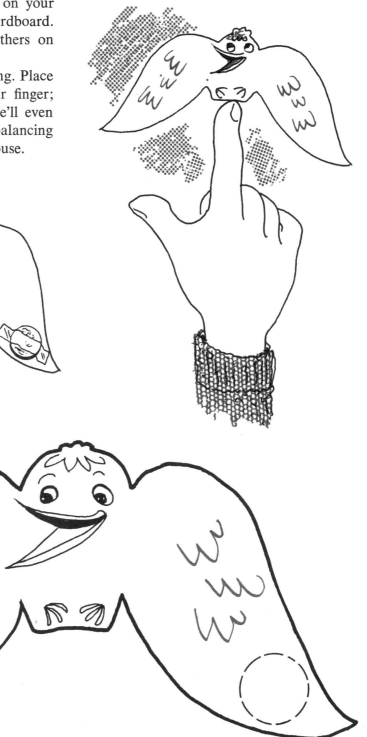

Back

13

Leaping Frogs Game

Trace and color these two frogs and paste them on cardboard. When dry, cut squares out and punch holes in top center. Cut two pieces of string about four feet long. Tie ends to legs of a chair or stool, 5″ from the floor. Tape securely in place. Thread frogs on strings. Each player holds a string with a frog on it.

Tilt frog square forward slightly, then jerk string and he will hop; let up on string and he will land. Repeat this, hopping the frogs toward the goal (chair leg). The frog square must touch the floor with each hop. Sliding along on the string is not allowed. The first frog to reach the goal wins.

Some Big Ideas For Small Boxes

Even the smallest empty boxes can be put to use. The boxes that contained mixes for puddings or gelatin, flip top cigarette boxes, small snack size cereal boxes or pill boxes are the bases of these constructions. Empty matchboxes and match folders are also used.

Please remember to wait until your parents have finished using the contents before you begin to make anything out of a box. Do not, ever, waste contents just to use the boxes.

Boxes of all sizes and shapes can be taped closed and covered with bright papers. Use them as building blocks.

Trim evenly around a box and staple on a strip of cardboard for a handle. Cover with pretty paper and you have a basket for party favors or just to keep little things in.

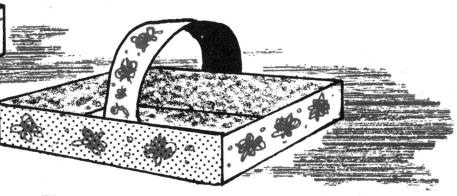

Make A Cuckoo Clock

For this project you will need two empty pudding or gelatin boxes, 2 pine cones, paper fastener, string and an ice cream pop stick.

Cut two pieces of string, one 4″ long, the other 7″ long. Poke two holes in the open end of one of the boxes. Tie a knot in each string and pull through holes, so two strings hang down. Paint box brown or cover with brown paper. Cut a 2″ circle from white cardboard. Draw a clock face on this circle with black felt pen. Cut out two hands. Use a paper fastener to hold hands together and insert through center point of clock face. Push paper fastener through side of box to put clock face into position. Open fastener inside box. Tape bottom (with strings hanging down) closed.

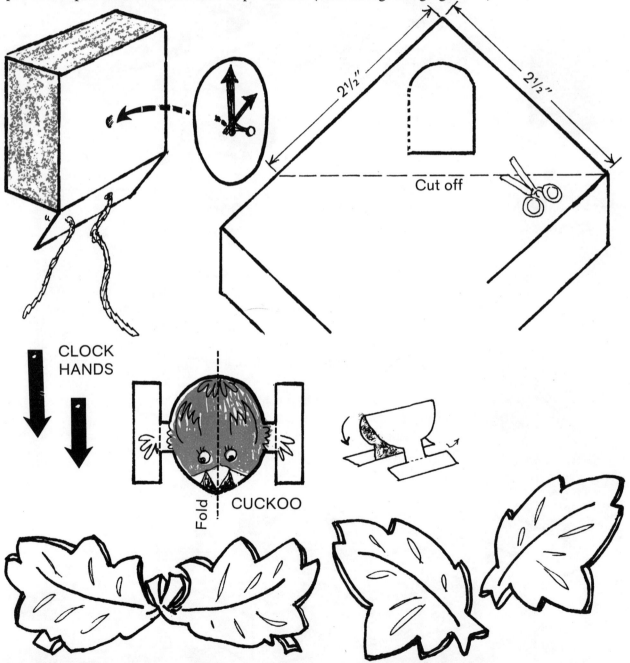

2½″   2½″

Cut off

CLOCK HANDS

Fold   CUCKOO

Now take box number two. Cut this box as shown to get a pointed piece for clock top. Color brown. Cut a door on one side, as shown. Fold side of door so it will open and close. In back of this piece of box, make a horizontal slit ⅜″ wide, directly opposite your door opening. Slide in the ice cream stick. Tie a 2½″ piece of string to inside of door. Attach string to the ice cream stick about ¾″ from the end, leaving about 1″ between door and stick. Now when you pull back the ice cream stick, the string should close the door. If not, adjust the length and position of string until it works.

Trace and mount leaves and cuckoo bird on cardboard. Cut out, fold bird as shown and tape to front end of stick. Attach two boxes together. Glue leaves into position. Tie a small pine cone to the end of each of the strings hanging from the bottom box.

Move hands to different hours, and move the cuckoo bird in and out by pushing the stick from behind.

Elec-Tricky Dancers

For this activity you'll need an empty pie or pastry box with a transparent piece in the top. Line the inside bottom of the box with dark blue paper. To make dancers use light colored tissue paper. Fold several pieces to approximately the size of the patterns below. Trace on patterns of the different dancers and cut out. This will give you many dancers. For stability, paste feet of each dancer onto a cardboard piece ¾″ long by ⅜″ wide.

Put dancers inside the box, replace top. Rub the cellophane top briskly to create static electricity. Soon your performers will dance. Have a ball.

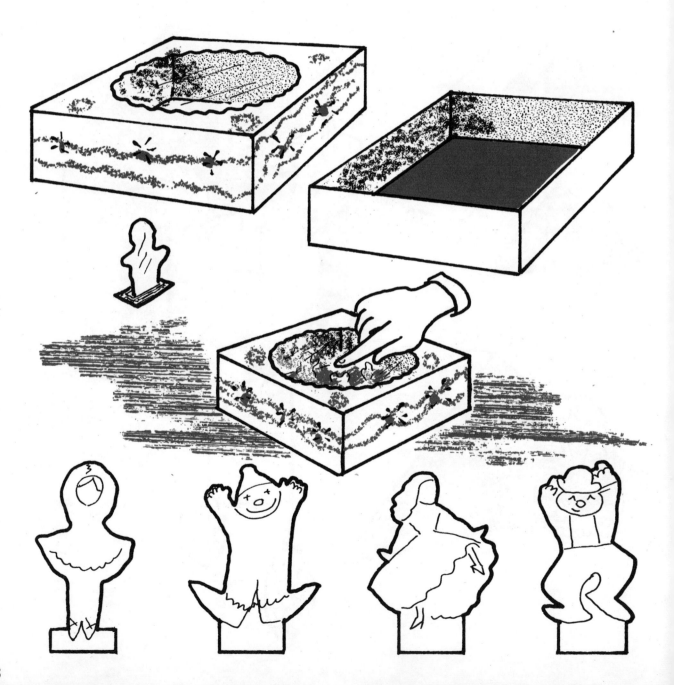

Make Them Roll

For this marble game, you'll need the lid of a sturdy box such as a candy or gift box, and a smaller pudding or cigarette box. Cut one flat side off of the small box. Cut two holes in the sides large enough for marbles to go into. Tape this smaller box into position as shown. Make number signs and tape in place.

If you want to make the game more difficult, put up a fence as shown.

Use three marbles or large wooden beads. Tilt cover to get them into holes. Take turns with a friend and keep score. Allow one minute for each turn.

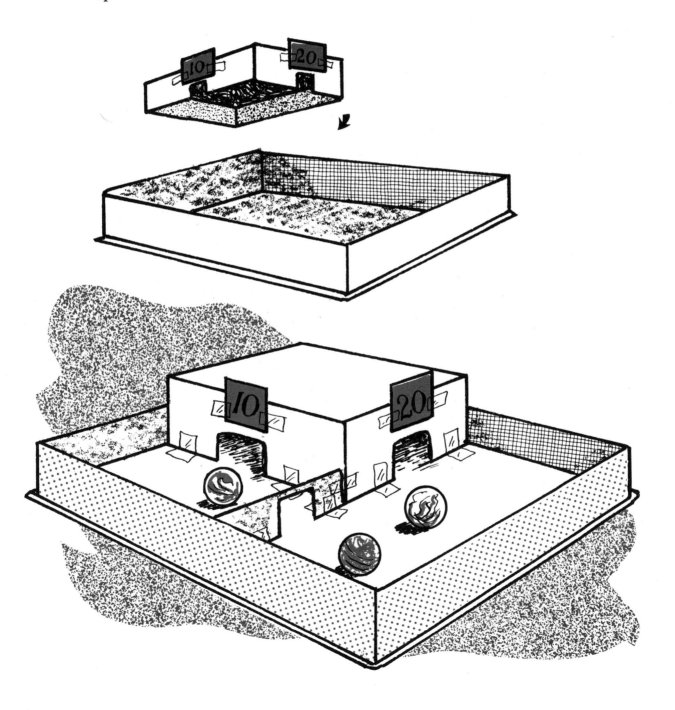

Make A Sicilian Cart

Use an empty gelatin or pudding box. Cut off one side, and cover with bright colored paper. To make shafts, cut two pieces of cardboard ½″ by 4″. Cover these with bright paper. Round the ends and punch holes in both ends.

To make wheels use four milk bottle caps. Cover these with gay paper. Punch hole at each center point. Use four paper fasteners to attach wheels to cart. On front wheels, insert paper fastener through cap, through hole in one end of shaft, and then into the side of cart. Repeat on other side for front wheel. Open fasteners to keep wheels in place.

Tie colored yarn into front holes of shafts, then tie around one of your toy animals that fits. Fill the cart with goodies.

Paper fastener

Owl Clip Holder

Use an empty kitchen match box, which is approximately 2½″ x 5″. Slide inside "drawer" out. Cover sides and back with black paper.Trace out owl head below and paste on cardboard. Color and trim carefully. Now mount on box. Add two paper clips to give dimension to his eyes.

For the drawer, cut a cardboard strip ½″ by 2¼″. Tape into position along bottom section. Using a black felt pen, color this barrier and ⅓ up the sides of drawer section. Then put the drawer back into the outside section (with owl face on it). Leave drawer sticking out approximately 1″ at bottom. Tape in place this way. Fill it with paper clips and you have a wonderful gift for your Dad to hang on the wall next to his desk.

Can You Match These for an Unusual and Practical Present

Empty match folders can be made into very attractive and handy miniature sewing kits for Mother's purse. Cover the outside with lovely paper or fabric. Notch as shown. Stick needles and pins into edges where the matches were. Wind black thread around the cover, through one set of notches. Do the same with white thread. Tuck cover in and your emergency sewing kit is ready to give to Mother.

How To Best Use Heavier Medium Size Boxes

Shoe boxes are very sturdy but can still be cut. Gift boxes come in various weights and sizes. If your mother gives permission, you can make things from these as well. Gift boxes usually have gay colors on the outside so you won't need to decorate them.

A Noise-Maker is easily constructed from a sturdy box with a cover. Add four rubber bands. Then pluck them and they will snap back noisily.

Boxes such as shoe boxes make excellent places to display your collections. To show a shell collection, paint inside blue and paste sandpaper on the bottom. If you have a rock collection, paste in bright colored labels for your specimens. Transparent food wrap around box will help keep out the dust.

3D Shoe Box Peek-o-Rama

Remove top and cut opening 1″ from side all around. Tape a piece of blue tissue paper on the inside.

Cut a small round hole in short side of bottom, as shown. Trace picture at bottom of opposite page and paste into position, opposite hole. Paste green paper to bottom of box. Draw a path in brown.

Trace and mount remaining pieces on cardboard. Cut out whatever figures you wish, to show a favorite fairy tale. Fold bases back and tape into position. While assembling your scene, check peephole frequently, making sure no figure hides another. Hang bat by black thread from the top.

When completed, replace top, hold under a light and peek in hole.

HORSE

WOLF

COW

WITCH

GIRL

BOY

PRINCE

Knock the Numbers Game

To make this game, you will need a large, long box, such as a dress or gift box. Cut end and fold as shown. Tape in position. You will need a piece of copper wire. To determine length needed, figure 3 to 4 inches for each side plus the width of your box. Slip wire through the spring of 3 clip clothespins. Cut three pieces of cardboard 1¼″ square. Cut numbers 5, 10 and 15 from an old calendar, or letter them on. Paste numbers to your cardboard squares. Clip these on clothespins. Bend wire to fit across the box, high enough so that the number squares barely miss box. Push wire ends through ramp and tape securely in place. Take turn rolling marbles down the ramp. Keep score. 200 points wins.

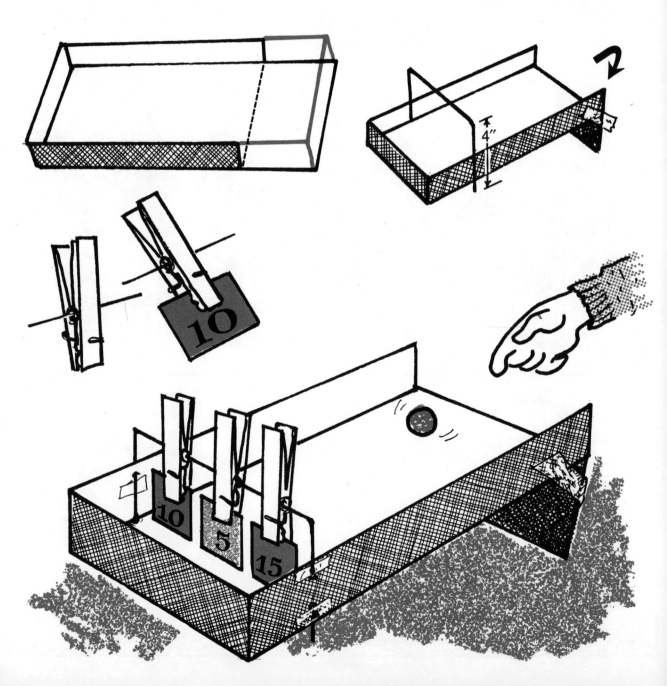

A Jolly Roger Ship

Use a shallow box. Trim top edges even. Cover with aluminum foil and tuck over top edges. Crush foil around corners to keep box waterproof.

Trace flag and sail. Use a soda straw for mast, punch holes in sail and thread mast through. Tape flag to top. Tape mast securely into position. Mount wheel on cardboard, cut out and tape to opposite end. Your Pirate ship is ready to sail the bounding main of your bathtub.

Scenic Diorama

Cut a shoebox down to about 2″ high all around or find a box with similar proportions. Any box with a solid separate cover will do. Set box top at back as shown. Tape in place. Find a lovely landscape in an old magazine to fit area at the back. Cut out and paste in place inside cover.

Line inside of bottom of box with aluminum foil. Fill box with sand. Now create a scene in front that will go with and look like part of picture in back. Use twigs, artificial flowers, little rocks, pebbles, shells, small mirror (for pond), toy figures, etc. If you have a snow scene, a layer of salt on top looks like snow. Use your ingenuity and see how good a scene you can make.

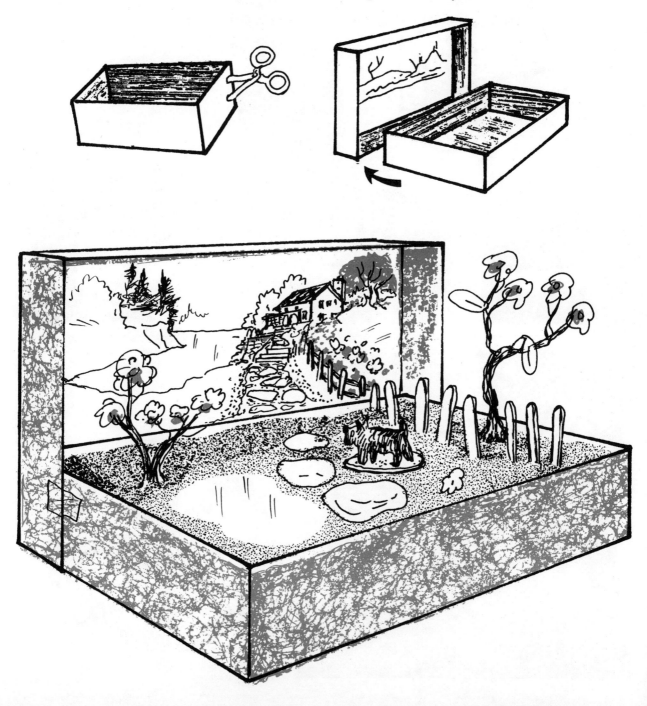

A Lion's Catch-All

Cover a sturdy box (such as a candy box) with tan paper. Cut 4 pieces of heavy twine about 6″ long. Tie knot on one end of each. Glue to the four corners of your box. Trim excess. These are your lion's legs. Trace face below on cardboard. Cut out. Cut another cardboard circle the same size. Cut twine for mane 1¼″ long; as many pieces as you like. Unravel them to look like mane. Paste around on back circle as shown. Now paste face circle over this. Glue or staple to front of box, add a rope tail. Fill your box with papers or pencils or whatever you like to keep.

Cage a Roaring Toy

Shoe boxes or similiarly shaped boxes make excellent cages for small stuffed animals. Cut a "window" in the cover, cutting ¾″ in from the edge on all four sides. Place box on side. Cage the toy animal. For bars, use colored straws long enough to extend slightly over top and bottom. Crush tips and tape into position.

Replace cover of box with window cut in it (this is the side you look through). The cover should cover the ends of straws and help hold them in place. Tape cover in place.

For name piece, cut cardboard 1″ x 5″ and paste it on at the bottom of the cage. Letter the animal's name. Make as many cages as you like for a circus or a zoo.

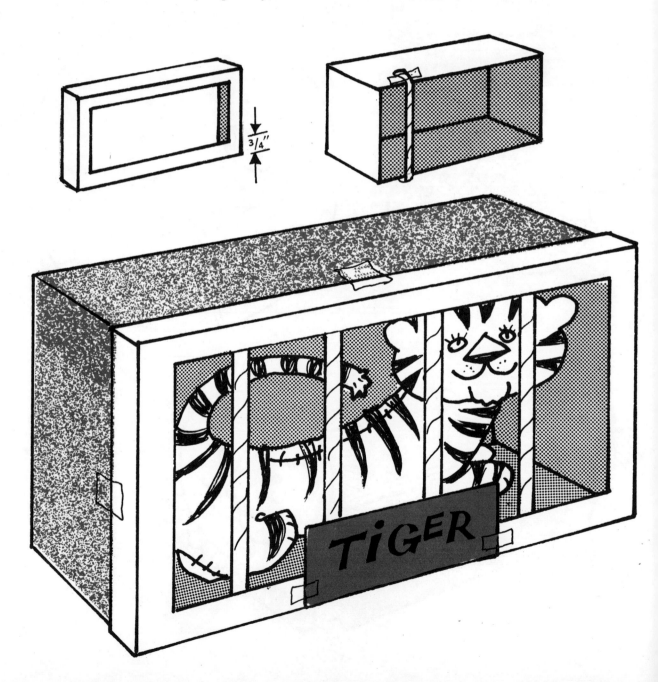

Make the Best of
Egg and Milk Containers and Food Trays

Milk containers come with either plastic or waxed surfaces. On the waxed surfaces you may need to apply liquid detergent to prepare the surface for painting.

Because they are waterproof they make attractive planters. Cut off one side, cover with pretty paper, and grow seedlings inside.

Egg cartons are often made of molded paper maché. These are easy to cut and color. All sorts of things can be made from this material.

Your local supermarket sells many items wrapped in pressed paper trays. Decorations can be painted or glued on so they make neat little trays to hold pencils or jewelry.

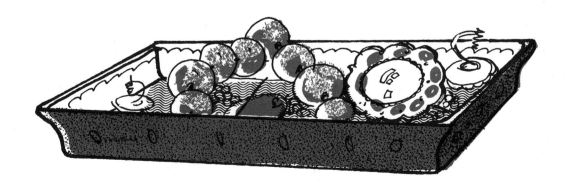

Be It Ever So Humble

Use a ½ gallon peaked milk carton. Glue colored paper around it on the four flat sides. Cut a hole 2″ in diameter halfway up from the bottom. Cut a small slit approximately 1″ below this hole. Insert twig for perch through front and slightly out the back, to hold it steady. Use another ½ gal. carton to make the roof. Cut a piece 4½ x 7½ using two sides as shown. Cover with different colored paper, fold in half and staple in position on top as shown. Staple on a cord or string and hang in a tree by your window.

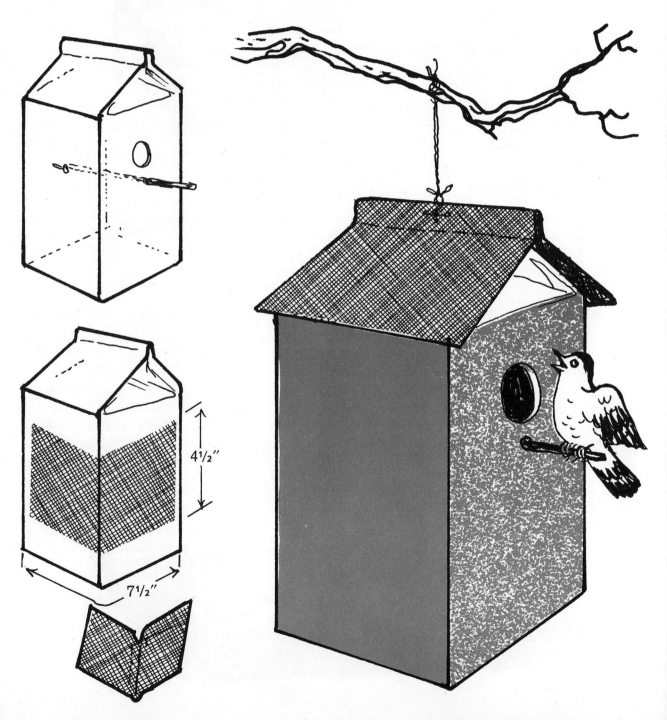

Make a Katchina Doll

You can make this colorful Indian doll from a quart size flat-top milk carton or a similar container. Clean and turn upside-down. Cut away on three sides 2″ from end. On remaining panel, draw feet shapes, and cut around them. Fold up.

Next, cut slit across top of doll (formerly base of carton) and 1″ down into sides. Cut cardboard the size and shape shown for headdress. Cover with bright colored paper. Use felt pens to draw designs. Slide headpiece into slit.

Cover body with bright paper, different from headdress. Draw on features. Paste on white apron-like piece. Use brightly colored pipe cleaners to make arms. Poke holes in corners of carton at proper height. Insert pipe cleaner and twist firmly to hold.

For rattles, use two toothpicks with a large bead glued to the end of each. Glue a tiny feather to other end. Attach to arms by twisting pipe cleaners around toothpicks. Add feathers to headdress. Now your Katchina Doll is ready to keep away evil spirits.

2″

5″

3″

HEADPIECE

Slit

Roxy the Rocking Horse

You will need two flat-topped quart milk cartons and 4 clip clothes pins. Paste tan paper on all four flat sides of one carton. Cut 4 holes in corners large enough for clothespin. Clip clothespins on for legs.

For head, use the other carton. Cut as shown and cover with tan paper. Draw mouth and eyes. Using ear pattern, cut two ears of brown cardboard. Cut slits in top corners of head, insert ears and tape in place. For mane, use yellow yarn and a large needle. Poke in and out, leaving 2" of yarn sticking out each time. Dab glue on inside, or tape the yarn to hold it secure. Now clip outside pieces at end of each loop. Fluff up to look like mane. Slip head onto body and staple in place. The front clothespins will also help hold it in place. Add string halter. Glue on a yarn tail. Cut saddle of bright paper and paste on. For rockers cut two pieces of cardboard 1" wide by 10" long and curve as shown. Glue to feet ends of clothespins. Now rock him gently.

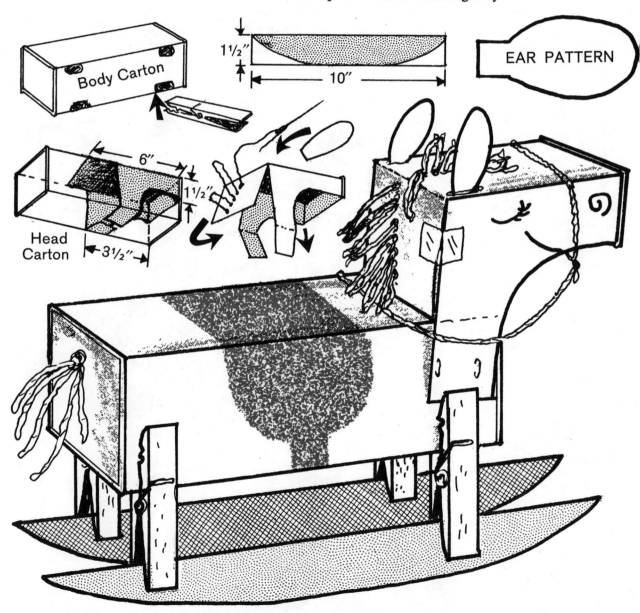

A Gas Pump

Use a flat-topped one-quart milk carton. Cover with bright red paper. Cut a piece of rope or string about 8″ long for "hose." Knot one end. Make a small hole in side of carton. Put other end of string down through the pouring spout and poke out through the hole. Pull "hose" through; knot should hold it in place. Crush a small piece of foil around tip for nozzle.

On back corner about halfway up, poke holes catty corner and insert end of a pipe cleaner. Twist on outside and make a loop for it to hold your "hose."

Stand up the pouring spout cover and paste or staple "Gas" signs on both sides. You can letter these or cut them out of old magazines. Paste a white panel in front for the gas indicators. Now you are in business to supply all of your toy cars and trucks.

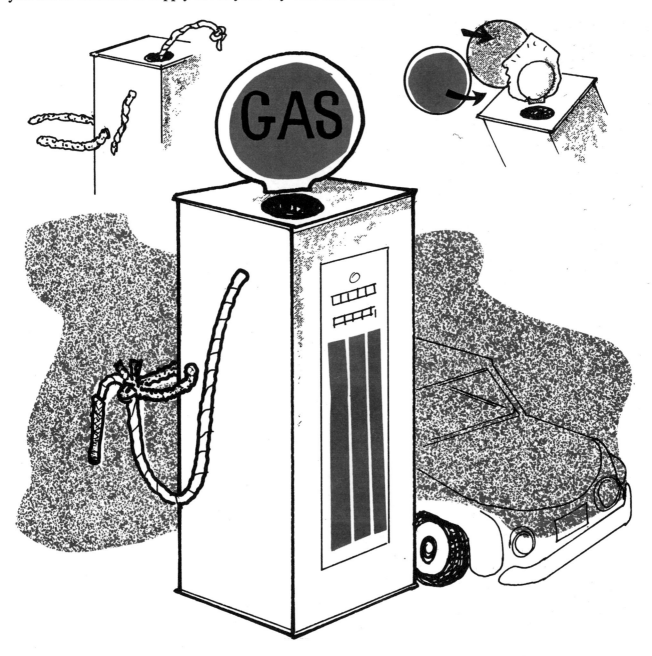

Japanese Wind Catcher

Use a peaked-top milk carton. Cover the four different sides with four different bright colors. Use cement if paste doesn't hold. Make a vertical cut at center of each panel. At top and bottom ends, cut ¾″ back on both sides of center cut. Fold these vertical panels, left side in, right side out. Punch hole in center of peaked top, tie a cord through and hang on a tree. It will twirl in the breeze. Make several wind catchers of different colors and hang them around your yard for a festive touch whenever there is a breeze.

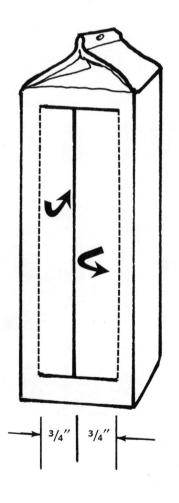

¾″ | ¾″

Row-Row-Row Your Boat

Use a peaked top one-quart milk container. Lay flat on side. Cut it all round 2″ from bottom as shown. Cut three seats from remaining piece, each 1″ wide. Staple in place.

For oarlocks, insert long end of a paper clip in between cardboard layers, one on each side. For oars, slip ice cream sticks through the paper clips. Now you are ready to row the boat in your bathtub.

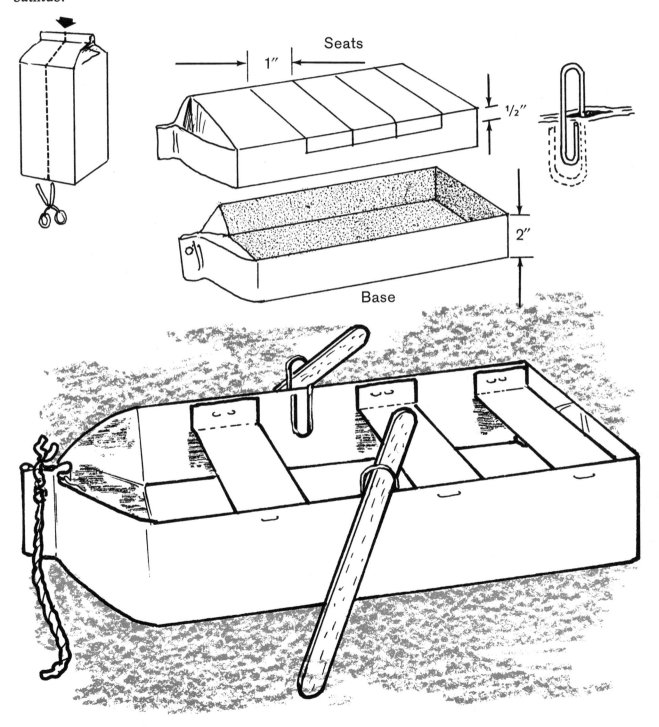

Egg Carton Bug-a-Boos

All sorts of wierd creatures can be made from pressed paper egg cartons.

A Caterpillar is made by cutting the carton in the middle lengthwise. This leaves six sections joined together. Trim neatly and paint. Add eyes and mouth. Antenna and tail piece are made of pipe cleaners.

A Bumble Bee is made of 3 sections. Cut wings out of white paper and staple into position. Paint face and stripes. Add pipe cleaner antenna.

For a Turtle, use one cup section only. Lay this on lid section of box and trace around it. Draw feet, head and tail. Cut out. Paste cup section to it and paint green. Draw eyes and shell decorations.

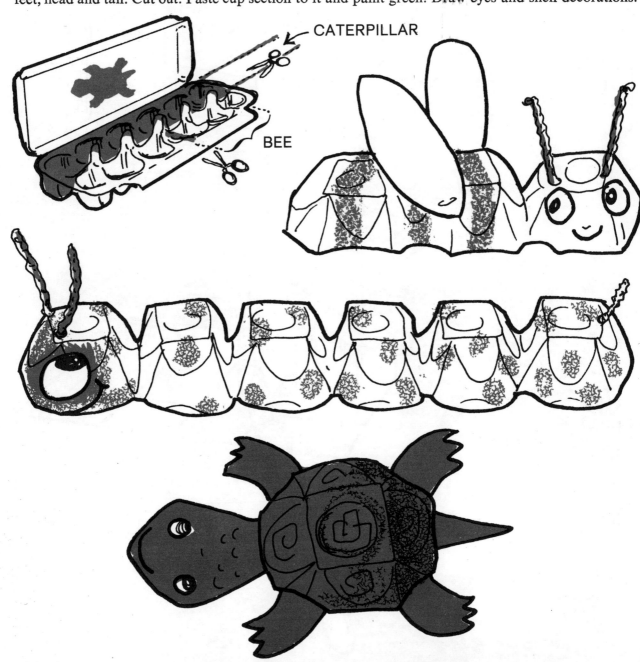

CATERPILLAR

BEE

Have a Tea Party

For the Nut Cup, cut out a 4 piece section of the egg carton. Spread paste inside of cups. Take 1″ strips of brightly colored crepe paper and work it down into the cups until the inside is neatly covered. Trim off excess. For handle, cut a strip from the lid section ½″ x 10″. Spread with paste and wind crepe paper around it. Staple handle in place.

Cups for your dolls can be made from one cup section. Paste on handles or use pipe cleaners. Decorate cups with felt pens. Using a compass, draw circle 2½″ diameter on lid of box. Cut out and decorate for saucers. Make as many cups and saucers as you like.

Make a Ring Toss Game

Use a fairly deep, pressed paper tray and a waxed paper tube for the pole. Cut a hole in center of tray so tube fits in tightly. Insert tube and tape on underside. Wind colorful crepe paper around tube and paste. To make base sturdier, tack edges of tray to a block of wood.

For rings use paper pie plates. Cut out center, decorate. Take turns tossing; keep score.

Mother's Kitchen Helper

Use a small shallow paper tray. Spread on paste and fit colorful crepe paper on inside. Crumple paper as you go, for added texture. Cut a cardboard piece the same width as the tray and about ¼ the height. Staple in place at the bottom. Decorate this with a lovely picture from an old magazine. Paint the remainder of the tray. To hang, punch two holes at top and run a cord through, then knot. Attach a cord on the side and tie a pencil at other end. Fill tray with scratch paper or a small pad.

Something Fishy

Cut five fishes out of cardboard using pattern below. Paint in eyes and numbers. Place a paper clip on nose of each.

Use a large pressed paper plate. Paint inside a light blue. Tie a two foot piece of string to a stick. Tie a small magnet to end of string. Take turns at "fishing". Keep score.

PATTERN

What To Do with Cardboards in the Round

Many special things can be made of round cardboard containers such as oatmeal and salt boxes. Covered with pretty fabric, an oatmeal box becomes a container for knitting yarn and needles.

Waxed paper, paper kitchen toweling, aluminum foil, food wraps and bathroom paper all have sturdy tubes inside which have many uses.

For playing Store make "Canned Goods" by cutting tubes in 2″ and 3″ lengths. Draw pictures of foods or cut them from old magazines and paste around tube pieces.

Round containers from such products as ice cream or cottage cheese are sturdy for storing things. Decorate and label. Or use a container to make a bank. Cut slit in top for coins. Decorate top and all around with gay designs, drawn or pasted on.

Heap Fun Totem Pole

Use a tube from wax paper that is 12″ long. Cover with bright yellow paper. For nose and eyes, use a single section from a pressed paper egg carton. Tape on. Using your imagination, draw eyes and mouths. Paint gay decorations. Cut ears from cardboard, make slits in side and insert ears into slits.

Cut a cardboard wing piece for the top. It should be about 8″ long and 2″ high. Decorate. Cut notches into top of tube and insert wing slits into these. Tape if necessary.

Insert completed totem pole into a pressed paper tray as described in last section for Ring Toss Game. Stand the totem on your bureau.

Jester for the Fun of it

Fold

ARM PATTERN

Again, use a 12″ tube. Color a 5″x7″ piece of white paper with checks and stripes. Paste around bottom part of tube. Paste pink paper on the remaining part. Paint on a face, belt and line for legs. Following patterns, cut arms and feet out of cardboard. Fold tabs of arms under and tape in place. Tape feet on. Dampen toes slightly and curl up. Cut a red bow tie and stick into place with a pin. Following pattern, cut cap out of colored paper or crepe paper. Attach jingle bells at tips if you have them. Glue around top of tube as shown.

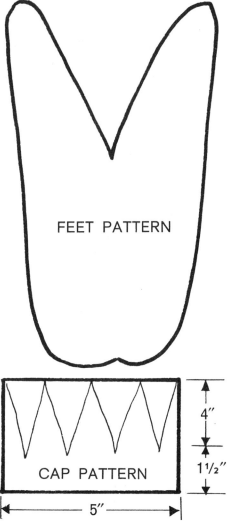

FEET PATTERN

CAP PATTERN

4″

1½″

5″

Snake Charmer Bracelet

Cut a 12″ tube along the spiral seam line. Then cut this in half so you have a strip about 1½″ wide. Cut about 2″ off each end to make a comfortable length for your arm. Make this a rounded cut, so the ends will look like the snake's head and tail.

Cut strips of green crepe paper and paste on all around, crinkling it as you go. Paint on some snake spots. Glue two beads to head for eyes. Now you are indeed a little charmer.

Rock-a-Doll Cradle

Cut a salt or oatmeal box as shown. For rockers use a sturdy piece of cardboard. To determine size, trace around end of round box. Draw a line across 1″ up from side of circle. Add ¾″ on this line outside of circle. Connect this point to bottom of circle forming curve, as shown. Cut two rockers this size. Cut notches.

Cut two slits in bottom sides of cradle. Slide rockers into position. Now your cradle will rock without tipping over. Use small pieces of fabric for pillow, coverlet and mattress. Put your doll to sleep.

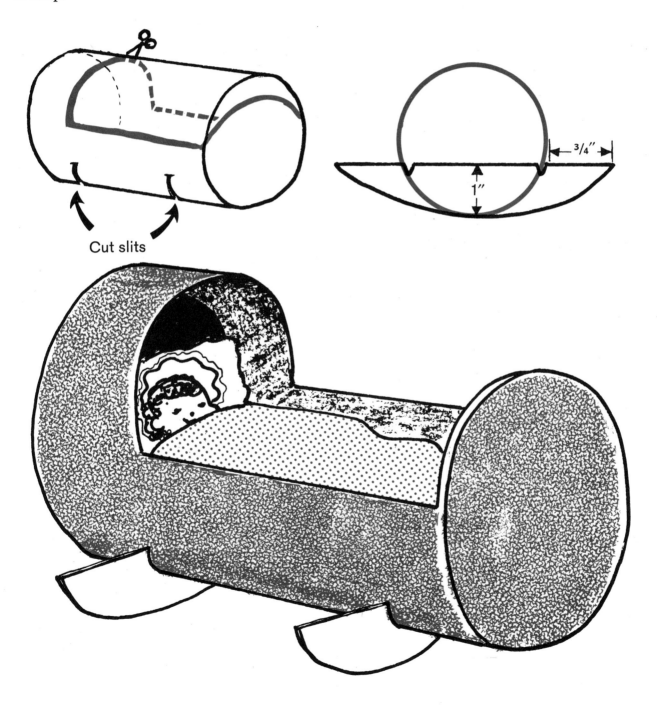

Cut slits

¾″

1″

Rob the Robot Puppet

His body is made of a 4″ long tube covered with aluminum foil. Glue on red paper gadgets. For legs use 4 pieces of soda straws, each 2½″ long. For arms use four pieces of soda straws, each 2″ long. For head, use a 2″ piece of tube, covered with white paper. Use felt pens to draw on features. For hat and shoulders cut 2 pieces of cardboard 3″ square. Cover with foil. Cut hands and feet from cardboard.

To string, follow instructions carefully. Use 3 pieces of yarn. No. 1 yarn begins at left foot, goes up through leg to body, down to right leg to foot. Tie at foot leaving sections loose and not touching. Yarn piece no. 2; knot at right hand, lead up arm, poke holes in side and put through chest, down left arm and tie knot at left hand leaving joints loose. No. 3 yarn; put down through body and tie to leg yarn as shown (in color) in drawing. Tie to arm yarn, up through shoulder piece, through a ½″ piece of straw for neck, up through head and hat. Tie a knot but leave yarn at top to hold by.

Now cut 4 pieces of string. Tie one to each knee, and one to each wrist. Hold the 4 strings and head yarn at top and see if you can make the robot walk and perform.

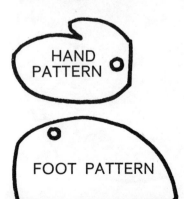

HAND PATTERN

FOOT PATTERN

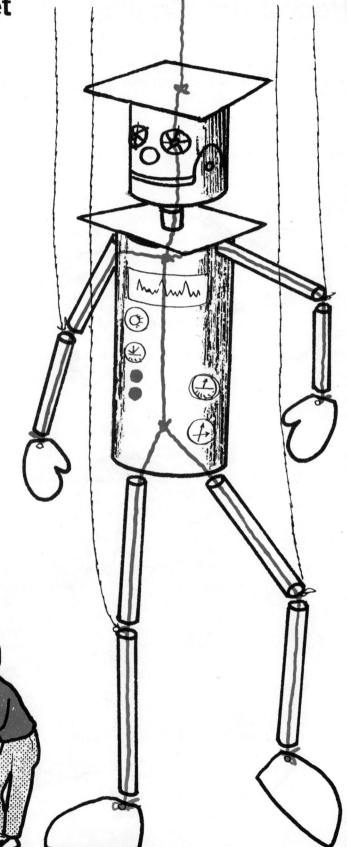

Make A Dandy Hanging Catchall

Use two empty round salt boxes. Glue ends together. Cut quarter section out lengthwise, as shown. Cover with gay fabric or paper. Bend a wire hanger to fit around boxes, adjust into position and tape together. Fill with clips or crayons or anything you like and hang on wall near your desk.

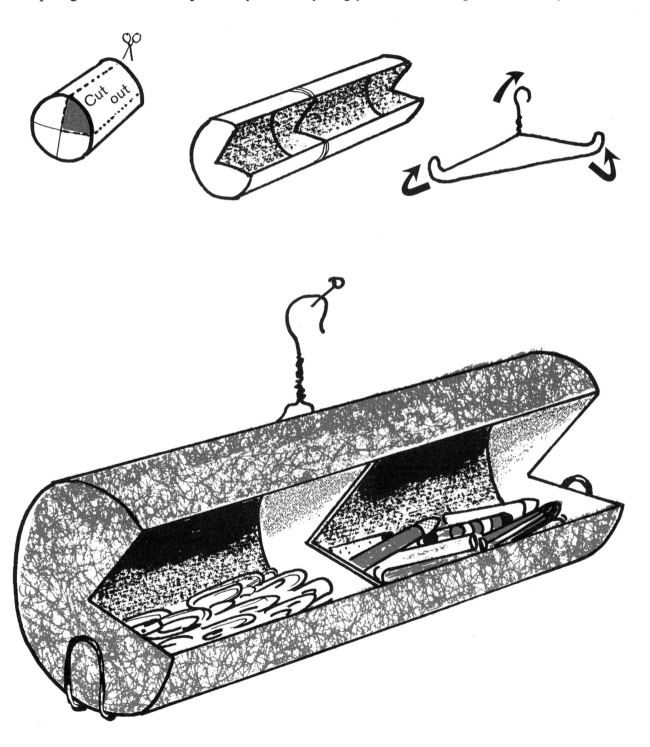

Owl on a Log

Trace and paste Owl on cardboard. Color and cut out. Curl him around.

For log, cut a piece of cardboard tube 2½″ long with tabs on top, as shown. Cover with brown paper. Insert owl's feet into slots to make him stand on log. Bend head down on dotted line. Bend tail up.

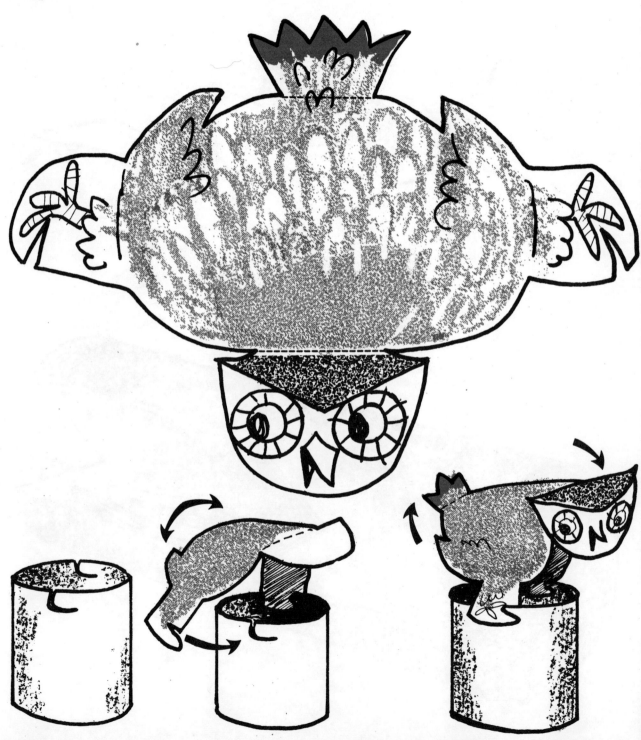

Jeremy the Giraffe

Trace head onto cardboard and color. Cut out and fold as shown.

Cut a 12″ tube as shown. Fold piece for back, over and down. Tape in place, Paint tube yellow with brown spots. Add a string tail. Staple back of head piece to top of neck to complete your giraffe.

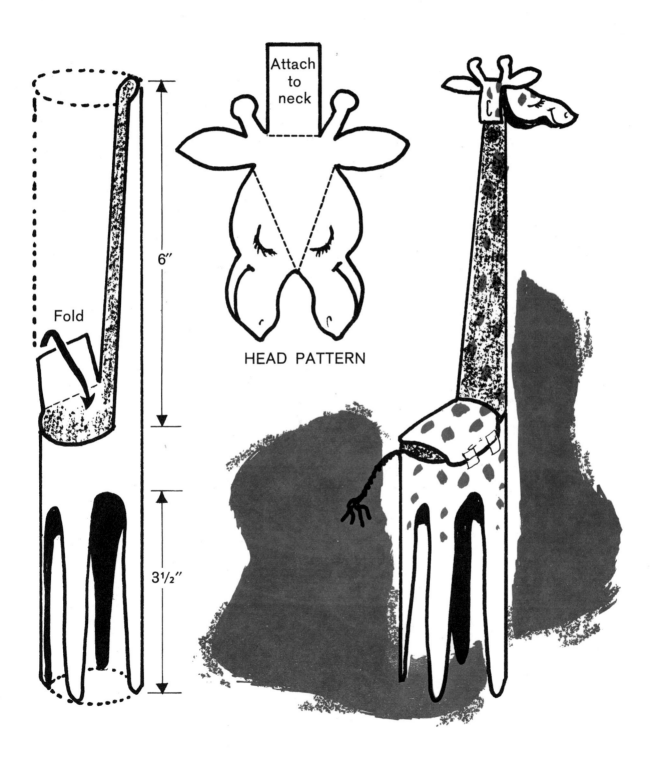

HEAD PATTERN

Esmeralda the Elephant

Trace and mount head on cardboard, cut out. For legs, cut a cardboard tube into four pieces, 2″ long. Insert them into an empty round salt box. Tape if necessary. For blanket, cut a piece of paper 6½″ x 3″. Decorate gaily and paste into place. Glue head on side as shown. Insert 2 pins with large round heads for eyes; they will help hold head in place. Add a string tail.

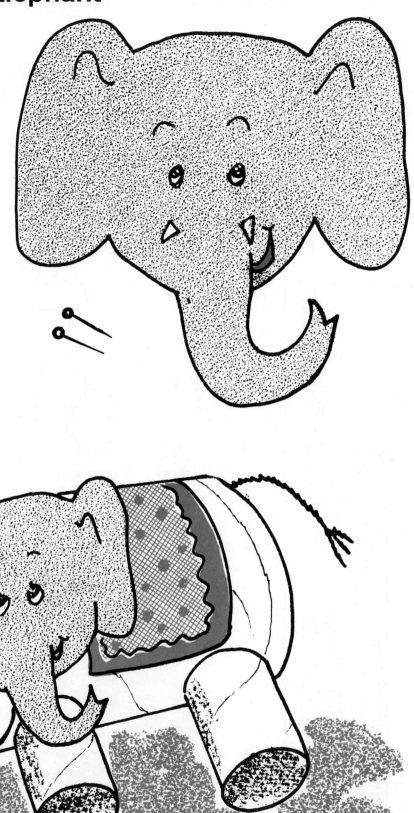

Make a Windmill

Cover a round salt box with red paper. Draw on the door and windows. Using a compass, draw a half circle 7¾" in diameter on red paper. Trace and cut out, curl around and tape. Tape in place at top of box.

Color and cut out pinwheel square on this page. Cut along dotted lines from corners only as far in as indicated. Put a pin through the holes in each corner and down through center x, to form pinwheel. Add a small bead on your pin; then push into side of box. Your windmill is complete.

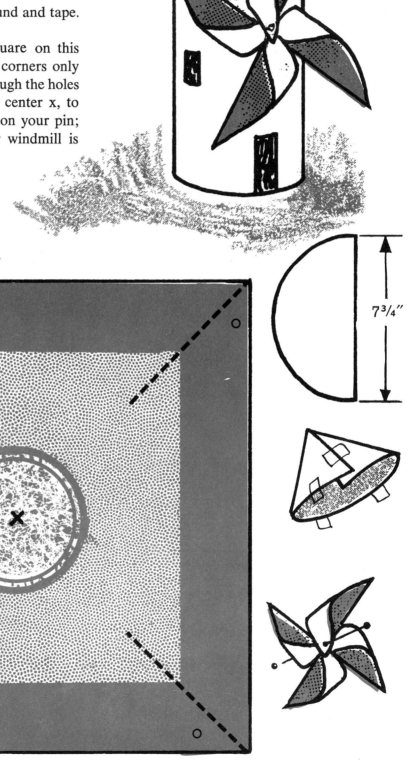

7¾"

Terry the Turtle

Use an empty round container such as a salt box or cottage cheese container. Measure 1½″ up from bottom. From this, draw up four feet, a head and a tail as shown. Cut out and fold pieces out. Cover with green paper or paint. Draw designs on shell. Glue on two black beads for eyes.

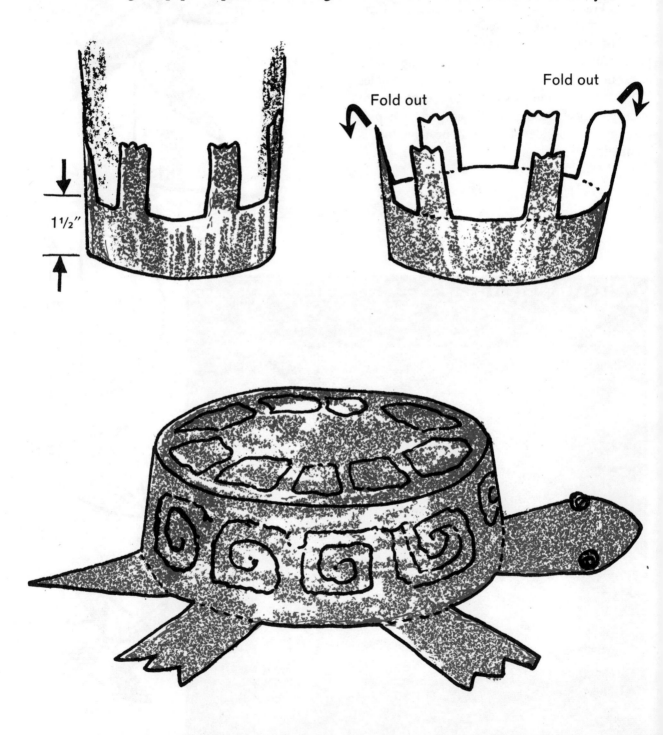

How to Make the Best Use of
Large Corrugated Cartons

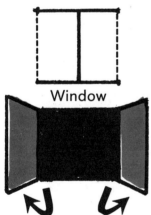

Window

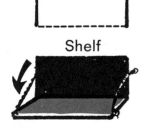

Shelf

Corrugated boxes can be obtained at most supermarkets. Extra large ones may come to your house on special occasions when you get a new appliance.

Heavy corrugated cardboard is difficult to cut. A scout knife or mat knife may be necessary. Be very careful in handling knives. Have your parents help you with the big cuts. Then you can decorate the boxes.

The biggest ones are fun to make into houses. If you cut an I shape, each side can be folded back to make shutters on your house. If you cut three sides and fold the fourth side at the bottom the piece becomes a shelf for a store. Add rope at the sides to keep it in place.

Large cartons that are not big enough to get into make good furniture for playing house. Tape flaps closed, turn over and paint on legs to look like a table. Or paint white and add four black circles for a pretend stove. A shelf type cut (like the one for the store shelf) can make an oven door.

Big boxes can become anything you like: a train, a car, a canoe or a caravan.

A Backyard Menagerie

Use large cartons that fit around you comfortably. Turn over; cut hole in bottom to fit you. Cut sides curved and ends across as shown. Leave beak for bird. Paint on features. To make shoulder straps, poke four holes around body hole, insert cord or ribbon. Adjust to fit your height, and tie knots inside. Cut ears out of sturdy cardboard and insert into slits you have made. Tape in place on inside. Repeat with bird's tail.

To make bunny tail, use white yarn, cut in 8″ lengths. Tie bunch tightly in middle and fluff up. Tape on box. If you want to make these animals more attractive, cover with colored papers first. Make several different animals using your imagination. Prance about your yard with your friends.

Marty-the-Martian Mask

A smaller corrugated box about 14″ wide makes a good mask. Tape flaps closed for back of mask. Cut off one end as shown, making a curve for your shoulders. Cut jaw piece from leftover piece, or use a similar size box. Cover box and jaw with aluminum foil. For eyes, cut two pieces of cardboard tubing, each 3″ long. Cut holes in box to see through, and fit tubes in place. Insert just far enough in to hold. Tape on inside. For nose, use an old jar top, covered with foil; tape in place. Antenna are pipe cleaners, crinkled and inserted in top of head.

To attach jaw, push a large paper fastener from inside out through the side of the jaw, and open fastener. Repeat on other side.

Paper
fastener

Make a Four Room Doll House

To make this four room house, cut a carton as shown, cutting down the center of each side and across. Swing the four sections around so that the four corners meet in center. Cut down to a height that looks best for rooms. Cut doors where desired. Glue the four sections together. Cover walls with pieces of old wallpaper, or paint them. Cut rugs out of old magazines. Decorate walls with small paintings or mirrors cut from old magazines. Your four room house is now ready for furniture.

Now Furnish your Home with Model Furniture

To make these pieces of model furniture, use small boxes such as those for gelatin, pudding mixes, or cereal snacks, or flip top cigarette boxes. Cut boxes as shown. Fold up back of chair, paste on fabric for seat and back. Tape arms will hold back in place. Cover boxes with paper, or paint them, to make table and bureau. Draw drawers on bureau.

Round table is made by gluing a jar top about 1¾″ across onto an empty spool. Glue marble textured paper on top. Paint spool white. Smaller round table is made of a milk bottle top glued to a cork. Paint. Flower pot is the top of a used toothpaste tube with tiny artificial flowers held in place by clay. Lamp is made with a button for the base, toothpick center and top of a squeeze-bottle detergent for shade. Glue together. Plates are buttons. You can probably find many other discarded things around your house that would be fun in your doll house.

TABLE

Fold up

CHAIR

BUREAU

ROUND TABLES

...and More Furniture

Again use small pudding-type boxes. For couch cut box lengthwise slightly wider than half. From remaining piece cut arms and back. Staple at end to hold in place. Glue fabric all around, trim off edges. Make a pillow by cutting a small piece of cardboard and covering it with fabric.

For bed, cut headboards to fit ends of box. Glue to each end. Cut soda straws the proper length, flatten slightly and glue to corners for posts. Paint head and foot boards. Use a piece of fabric for spread.

For stove, cut box to the right proportions, cover with white paper and draw on knobs, burners, etc.

Use your own imagination and make as many pieces of model furniture as you like by applying these general instructions.

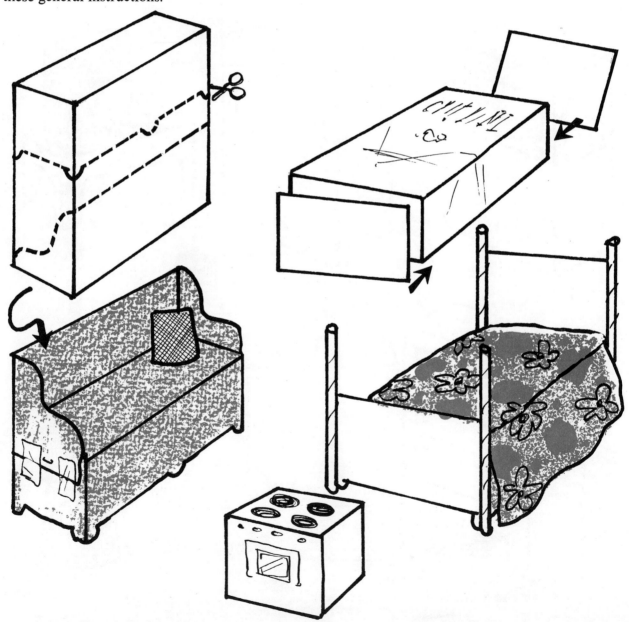

Presto! Your Four Room House Becomes a Shopping Center

Make store signs and letter them. Cut slots in sides and slip into slots you make in corners. Paste small pieces of crepe paper to string for decorations. Use your toy cars for an auto showroom. Plastic animals can be "sold" in a Pet Shop. Make the furniture for a Toy Furniture store. For a Grocery Store make counters by cutting small boxes down to size. Make a cupboard as shown. Cut pictures of foods from old magazines and paste into place. Use your imagination and see what kind of store you'd like to make.

Camelot Castle

By now you must have quite an asortment of boxes, all shapes and sizes. Now let's make a castle, and a miniature town.

The body of the castle is a large corrugated box. Smaller boxes of all types and sizes make the side sections. Cover with gay paper. Cut squares for doors and windows from black paper. Paste in place. For drawbridge, tape string to castle and down to a small flat box cover.

For turrets, use round containers or tubes. Cover these with paper. To make roofs, cut a half circle of paper. To figure diameter of circle, wrap a a piece of string around top of round box. Use a compass to spin your half circle. Cut out and tape one end to round box. Wrap top around and tape to hold in place. Add trim.

Tape a red flag to a long hat pin and stick in box. Front posts are small candles stuck into empty spools. Tape flags to wicks. Set all units in place. Now your castle is ready for your toy King, Queen and Knights.

Main City, U.S.A.

Again you'll need boxes of different shapes and sizes. Use an oatmeal box for a silo. Cover with red paper, cut a white roof as described on last page for turrets. To make a barn, cut an oatmeal box in half and paste onto a rectangular box the proper size to fit it. Cover with red paper, draw windows and doors.

For church, use an egg carton with interlocked sections, cut in half (half dozen size). Cover with colored paper, add windows and doors. For steeple, use tube cut to height desired. Cover with paper, add a round roof and draw bell.

Use different sizes and shapes of boxes and lots of imagination to make stores, shops and homes for your Main City. Small boxes make chimneys on bigger boxes. Several sizes put together look like stores or factories.

All The World's a Stage

Use two large corrugated cartons approximately the same width. Turn both boxes upside down so open end is on the bottom. Use taller one for bottom of stage. Cut a fairly large hole in top of bottom box and an opening in the back. This is where you will be able to put your arms through to work your puppets.

For the top box, cut out front and paste on fabric for curtains. Cut hole in back to look through as you move your puppets. Glue or tape the boxes together. Decorate gaily. Now you can entertain your friends with a hand puppet show.

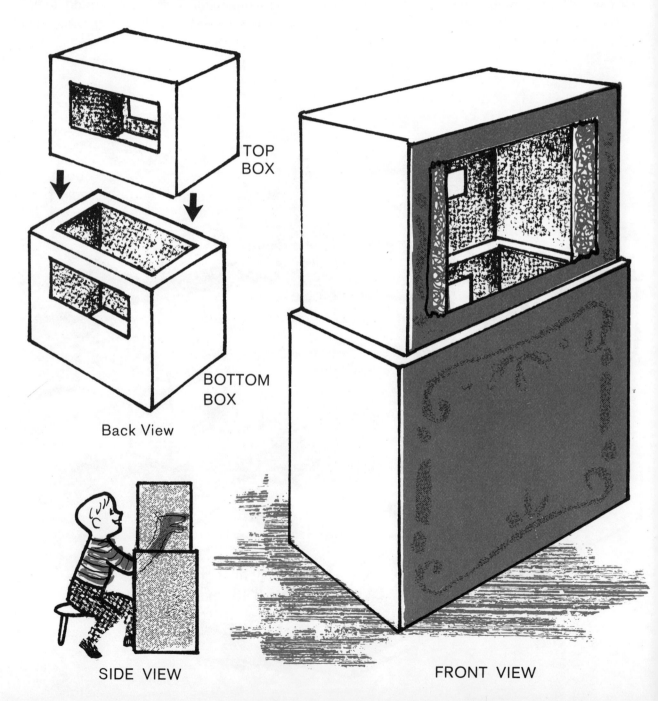

TOP BOX

BOTTOM BOX

Back View

SIDE VIEW

FRONT VIEW